U0917474

印象上黄

中国传统村落

THE IMPRESSION OF SHANGHUANG

CHINESE TRADITIONAL VILLAGES

王祝兴　高光荣 / 主编

中国环境出版社 · 北京

图书在版编目（CIP）数据

印象上黄 : 中国传统村落 / 王祝兴，高光荣主编. -- 北京 : 中国环境出版社, 2017.12

ISBN 978-7-5111-3367-0

Ⅰ. ①印… Ⅱ. ①王… ②高… Ⅲ. ①村落－武义县－摄影集 Ⅳ. ①K925.55-64

中国版本图书馆CIP数据核字(2017)第244410号

责任编辑　陈金华
责任校对　尹　芳
装帧设计　彭　杉

出版发行　中国环境出版社
（100062 北京市东城区广渠门内大街16号）
网　　址：http://www.cesp.com.cn
电子邮箱：bjgl@cesp.com.cn
联系电话：010-67112765（编辑管理部）
010-67113412（第二分社）
发行热线：010-67125803 010-67113405（传真）
印　　刷　北京中科印刷有限公司
经　　销　各地新华书店
版　　次　2017年12月第1版
印　　次　2017年12月第1次印刷
开　　本　787×1092 1/12
印　　张　15.5
字　　数　12.8千字
定　　价　138元

编委会

EDITORIAL BOARD

小荷才露尖尖角

THE LITTLE LOTUS JUST SHOWS ITS TINY BUD

序

乡村，五千年中华民族文化之根；乡愁，摸不着，看不见，自古至今都能牵得起离乡游子的家国情怀。随着工业化和城市化浪潮滚滚涌来，乡村原有的恬静被打破，人们不断地涌向“水泥森林”——城市。乡村，失去了往日的勃勃生机，渐渐衰败、没落。

然而，在浙江武义依然有这样一个村，她与周围村落颓败荒废的景象截然相反，仍看得见炊烟在晨光中、在日暮里袅袅升起，仍看得见儿童在田野里追着蜻蜓嬉闹，仍看得见春燕叼衔黄泥结喙楼梁景象，仍听得见鸡鸣犬吠在空阔山野中远远传来。这个村，就是中国传统村落——上黄村。

上黄，地处浙西南山区，海拔 1050 米，是瓯江水系发源地之一，是武义南部海拔最高的山村，是一个有着近400人口的千年古村落。上黄先人智慧将幢幢土楼依山而建，层叠楼垒，耸立蓝天，四周环翠；白云窗前过，雁声伴儿啼；故被人称为“江南版布达拉宫”。因村人仍保持千年来的生活习俗，又称为“云中部落”。自古以来，上黄的风景引人瞩目。上黄《宗谱》里的《王氏地舆记》这样描述上黄：“踞崇山峻岭之险，路远瀍涧，成茂林修竹之趣。脉迢迢而耸秀，成蓬岛境；翳翳而盘旋，别一洞天。碧峰映照，飞霞与落日交辉；岚光四射，秋月并峦影齐明；犬啼霜涧，偕鹿鸣而俱呦；鸡唱云间，对鸟语以争清。诚幽人之所寄托，达士所依凭。”

上黄，遍及华夏的工业化浪潮在这里受阻回旋。这与上黄人“父母在不远游”口口相教的家风分不开，更与千年“忠孝”的文化积淀分不开。北宋年间，上黄人的先辈发现了这个世外桃源，迁徙来这里落脚生根，繁衍后代。他们敬宗修庙，合修学堂，建涵排水，开山造田，筑桥修路，历经宋、元、明、清、民国。村里的一片瓦、一条青石板，都是历经沧桑，都是一段文字，都是悠悠历史。

上黄，耕读传家，历代人才辈出。特别是到了近现代，有积极投入解放战争的热血青年，有知名科学家，有事业成功的企业家，他们热心公益事业，不忘桑梓之情，出资出力，以保护古村落传承乡村文化为自豪。随着上黄“江南布达拉”美名的远扬，全国不少专家学者、传统村落保护人士、旅游爱好者倾注了对上黄村的关爱和呵护。

《印象上黄》分五大部分，即江南布达拉、自然风光、千年历史、文化传承和名传八方。在这些帧帧精美照片中除了可以欣赏上黄的自然美以外，还可以阅读出上黄千年历史、上黄的沧桑，也是当今中国乡村变化的缩影。

愿上黄宗祠，永世相传，芳流不朽，天长地久。

愿上黄古村，与时俱进，恩泽不竭，地久天长。

王祝兴

记于 2017 年 11 月 18 日

PREFACE

Villages are the foundation of 5000-year Chinese culture. Nostalgia is yet intangible but still can make the wanderers long for the homeland. However, the industrialisation and urbanisation broke the peacefulness in countrysides and villagers keep flooding into the "concreate jungles". Villages have lost its thriving vitality and gradually vanish.

However, there is still a well-kept village in Wuyi, Zhejiang. You can still see the most traditional scenes in here-wisps of smoke rising from the village chimneys; children chasing after dragonflies in the fields; swallows carrying mud to build nests; barking of dogs and cocking of chickens come from vast mountains... This is what is called a traditional Chinese village—Shanghuang village.

Shanghuang, an ancient village, has a population of 500 and locates in the southwest mountain area of Zhejiang with an altitude of 1,050 meters—the village with the highest altitude in the South of Wuyi. The ancestors of Shanghuang used their wisdom to build the mud houses along the hills, layer by layer, house by house, coupling with blue sky, surrounding by green plants. Imagine you are in the village, you can see the clouds float past windows, and hear the sound of wild goose accompany by infants'cries. Therefore,

Shanghuang is also known as "the Potala of the southern region of the Yangtze River". Moreover, because the villagers still keep the customs from thousands of year ago, it is also known as "the tribe in the cloud".

Shanghuang, the waves of nationwide industrialisation were blocked here. The reason why is closely related to the Shanghuang's culture of "when parents are alive, one should not travel far", and moreover, the cultural heritage of being "loyal and filial". During the Southern Song Dynasty, the ancestors of Shanghuang discovered this utopian paradigm and settled here. They built temples, schools; developed drainage systems; cut into mountains and reclaimed croplands; constructed bridges and roads. The village has been through Song, Yuan, Ming, Qing Dynasties and the Republic of China—every tile and every quartzite have gone through the vicissitudes of history. The everlasting natural beauty of Shanghuang has impressed many people since thousands of year ago. The *Wang's Di Yu Ji* in Shanghuang's Genealogy describes the beauty of Shanghuang as "mounting among the danger of high mountains and lofty hills; travelling a long distance and in-between rivers; enjoying the amusement in the flourishing woods and tall bamboos. The mountains extend far with flourish trees, forming a green paradigm. Above the green mountains, roseate clouds and the radiating sun bring out each other. The moonlight shines through mists, irradiating the mountains. The barking of dogs accompanies the bleating of dears; the crowing of roosters attends the tweeting of birds. It holds dreams of hermits and the ambition of the elites".

Shanghuang has cultivated many outstanding people, especially in recent decades, Sueh as soldiers who devoted themselves to War of Liberation, well-known scientists and successful entrepreneurs. Shanghuang's people are all warm-hearted and proud of being a part of the heritage. They have been investing in the preservation of Shanghuang. Moreover, as the reputation of "the Potala of the Southern region of the Yangtze River" spreads far, many of the scholars and protectionists of traditional villages have dedicated their love and care to Shanghuang.

The Impression of Shanghuang is divided into five parts: the Potala of Southern China, the Natural beauty, thousands of year history, the traditional cultural inheritance and circulation in all directions. You will enjoy the natural beauty of Shanghuang from the exquisite photos and read the stories of Shanghuang which are also an epitome of the transition of Chinese villages.

Wish the ancestor temple of Shanghuang, be forever, long-lasting and enduring as the universe.

Wish the ancient village of Shanghuang, be advanced with times, continuous with grace and everlasting.

Wang Zhuxing

November 18, 2017

荷美绽放

THE BEAUTIFUL LOTUSES ARE BLOOMING

目　录

CONTENTS

江南布达拉

THE POTALA OF THE SOUTHERN CHINA

九曲十八湾
——通往上黄古村的盘山公路

NINE CURVES AND EIGHTEEN TURNS
– THE WINDING ROAD TO SHANGHUANG VILLAGE

江南布达拉
——镶嵌半山腰的古村落

"THE POTALA OF THE SOUTHERN REGION OF THE YANGTZE RIVER" – THE VILLAGE IN THE HILLSIDE

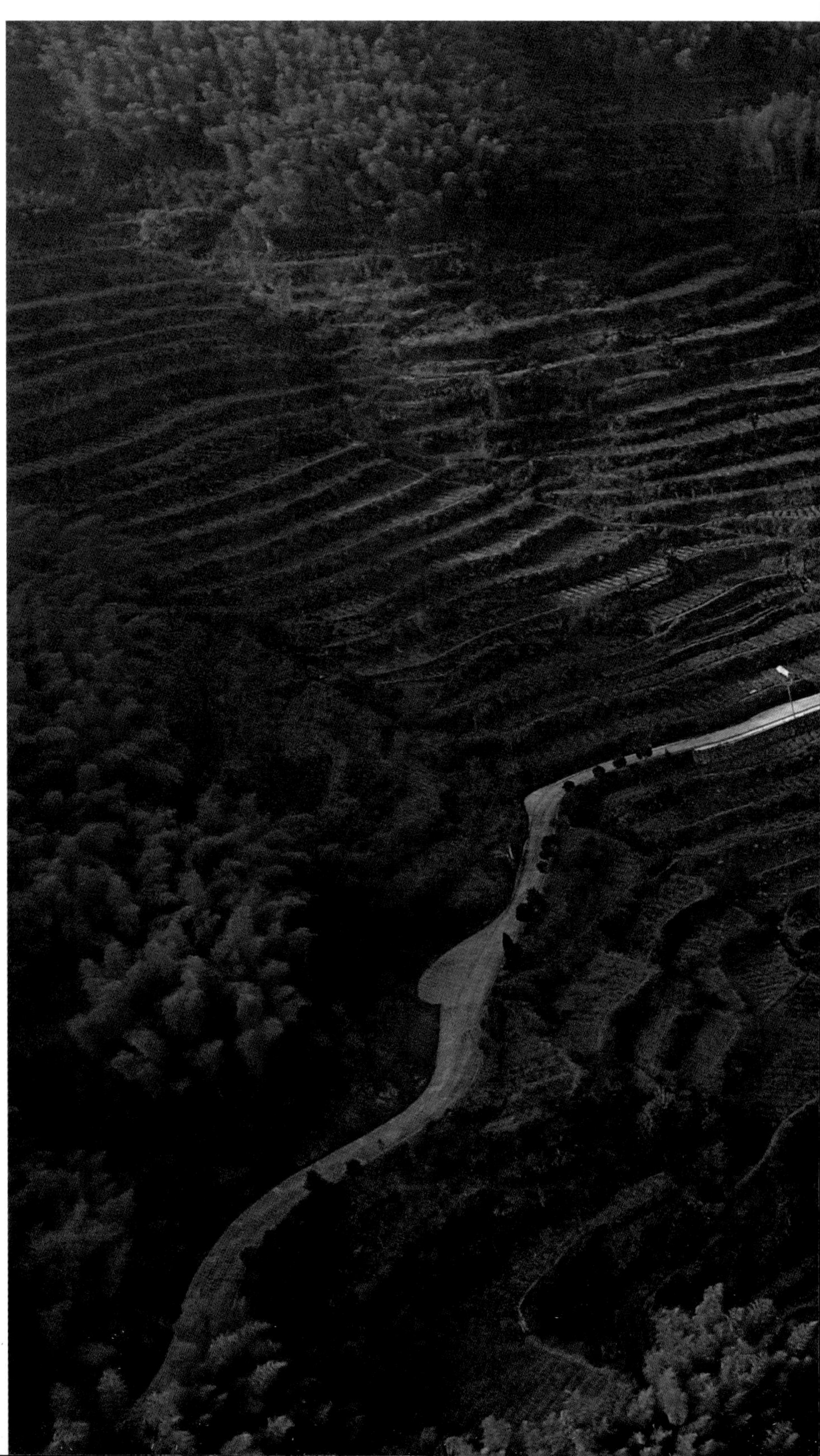

鸟瞰上黄

A BIRD'S-EYE VIEW OF SHANGHUANG

山村翠谷
THE VILLAGE WITH GREEN MOUNTAINS

雨后初霁

THE SCENE AFTER THE RAIN

炊烟初起

WISPS OF SMOKE FROM CHIMNEYS

鸟瞰上黄

A BIRD'S-EYE VIEW OF SHANGHUANG

俯瞰上黄
BIRD'S EYE OF SHANGHUANG

上黄雪景

THE SNOWSCAPE OF SHANGHUANG

冰雪之路

SNOW-CAPPED ROAD

上黄早晨
MORNING OF SHANGHUANG

老宅
OLD HOME

一缕阳光
A RAY OF SUNSHINE

古村满月

THE VILLAGE UNDER THE FULL MOON

古村之夜

THE NIGHT OF THE ANCIENT VILLAGE

古村民屋

HOUSES IN THE ANCIENT VILLAGE

古村民舍

HOUSES IN THE ANCIENT VILLAGE

人民公社万岁

自然风光

NATURAL BEAUTY

天池

小瀑布

古村仙境
THE WONDERLAND OF THE ANCIENT VILLAGE
山澗小溪細水長流

上黄大峡谷
THE GRAND CANYON OF SHANGHUANG

山花灿烂大毛山

DA MAO MOUNTAIN WITH FLOWERS IN FULL BLOOM

竹乡
THE BAMBOO VILLAGE

竹海情深
THE SEA OF BAMBOOS

古道森林

AN ANCIENT PATHWAY IN THE FOREST

杉树桥

CEDAR BRIDGE

上黄古道

千年古道

AN ANCIENT PATHWAY

星光灿烂

STARRY NIGHT

初冬之夜

A NIGHT OF EARLY WINTER

古村幕色

THE ANCIENT VILLAGE UNDER THE TWILIGHT

雪埋竹海

THE BAMBOO SEA IN THE SNOW

踏雪

TAPPING SNOW

雾霭古村

VISITING THE MISTY VILLAGE

天池
THE SKY POND

秋红

THE AUTUMN RED

竹林观音庙
GUANYIN TEMPLE IN THE BAMBOO VILLAGE

日出宣平
THE SUNRISE IN XUANPING

金霞沐村

THE VILLAGE UNDER THE SUNLIGHT

上黄毛山
THE MAO MOUNTAIN OF SHANGHUANG

毛山天池

THE SKY POND OF MAO MOUNTAIN

红霞尽染
THE SUNSET GLOW IN SHANGHUANG

九曲回肠
THE TWISTY ROAD

双猴拜僧

TWO MONKEYS WORSHIP MONK

送子洞

THE CAVE FOR PRAYING FOR SONS

胞胞杉

TWIN TREES

古村朝霞

MORNING GLOW IN THE VILLAGE

云中部落
THE TRIBE IN THE CLOUD

千年历史

THOUSANDS YEARS' HISTORY

雾腾上黄

CLOUDY SHANGHUANG

村庄巷道
ALLY IN THE VILLAGE

地下水渠
UNDERGROUND CANAL

宗祠重光 欢迎光临
上宗祠
王氏宗祠
上宗祠
下宗祠
閻王廟

觀音廟
祀殿
西坑祖廟
文武宮
THE MAP OF THE ANCESTRAL TEMPLES IN SHANGHUANG
上黃廟祠分布圖

王德用宗祠（THE ANCESTRAL TEMPLE OF WANG DEYONG），修建于 1814 年，至今 200 余年。志载：嘉庆年间，王德用氏族后裔合众商议：自元、明清以来，谱牒历经编辑而宗祠未得剏作。故以妥先灵之款式，序昭穆长次为目的，合族出资修建祠宇。

王荣宗祠（THE ANCESTRAL TEMPLE OF WANG RONG），嘉庆年间，王荣氏族后裔合族商议：先祖自宋元丰年间（1078-1085）迁至上黄，历数十世未建立祠宇，先灵无以安妥，子孙无以致敬，于是合众出资在 1796 年修建至今 200 余年。

王荣族谱

THE PEDIGREE OF WANG RONG

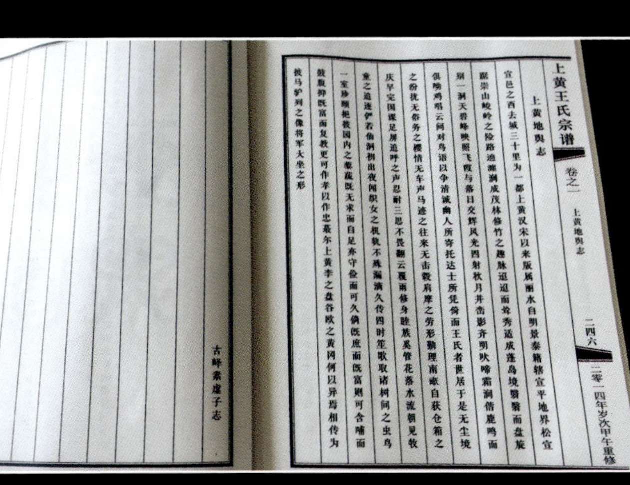

上黄王氏宗谱　卷之一　上黄地舆志　二四六

上黄地舆志

宣邑之西去城三十里为一都上黄汉宋以来版属丽水自明景泰籍辖宣平地界松宣
踞崇山峻岭之险路迪濂涧成茂林修竹之趣脉迢迢而耸秀适成蓬岛境翳翳而盘旋
别一洞天碧峰映照飞霞与落日交辉凤光四射秋月并岙影齐明吠啼霜涧偕鹿鸣而
俱嘹鸡唱云间对鸟语以争清诚幽人所寄托达士所凭倚而王氏者世居于是无尘境
之纷扰无俗务之樱情无车声马迹之往来无击毂肩摩之劳形勤理南畝自获仓箱之
庆早完国课足屏追呼之声忍耐三思不畏翻云覆雨修身睦族奚管花落水流顿见牧
童之追逐俨若仙洞初出夜闻织女之机轨不殊漏滴久传四时笙歌取诸树间之虫鸟
一室弦颂艳播园内之蔬蔬既无求而自足亦守俭而可久倘既庶而既富则可含哺而
鼓腹抑既富而复教更可作孝以作忠蕞尔上黄李之盘谷欧之黄冈何以异焉相传为
披马驴列之像将军大坐之形

二零一四年岁次甲午重修

古峙素虚子志

上黄王氏宗谱　卷之一　上黄地舆志　二四七

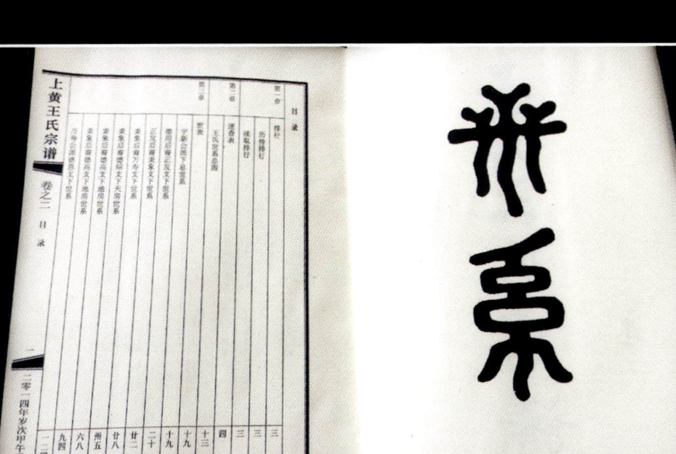

上黄王氏宗谱　卷之一　目录

目录

一

二零一四年岁次甲午重修

王氏宗譜

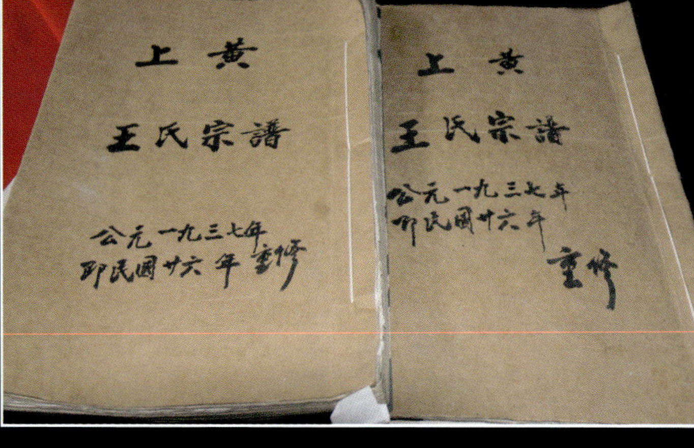
上黄
王氏宗譜
公元一九三七年
即民国廿六年 重修
上黄
王氏宗譜
公元一九三七年
即民国廿六年
重修

王氏宗譜
副本
王氏宗譜
副本
王氏宗譜
副本

上黄王氏宗譜
公元二千零六年岁次丙戌重修

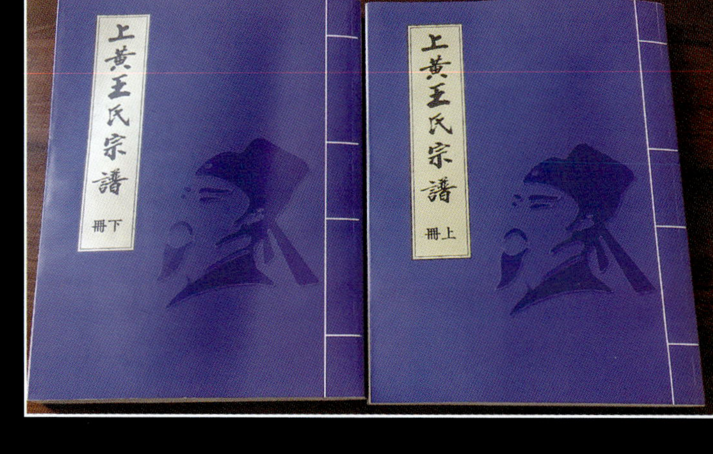
上黄王氏宗譜
册下
上黄王氏宗譜
册上

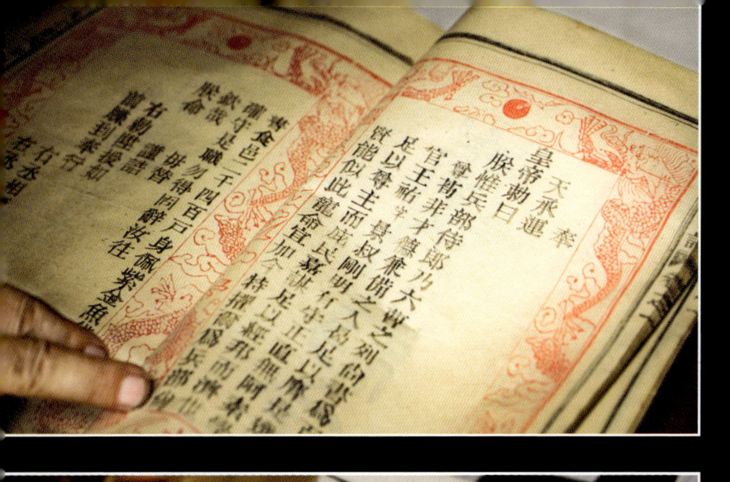
奉天承運
皇帝勅曰
朕惟兵部侍郎乃大司馬之列

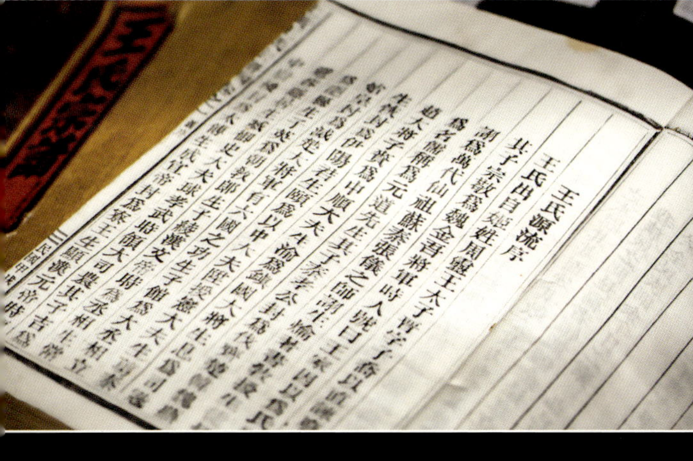
王氏源流序

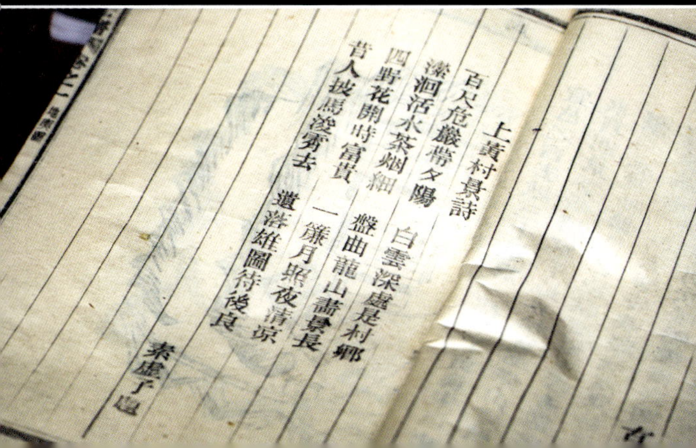
上黃村景詩
百尺危巖帶夕陽　白雲深處是村鄉
潆洄活水茶烟細　盤曲龍山畫景長
四野花開時富貴　一簾月照夜清凉
昔人披馬淩霄去　遺跡雄圖待後良
素虛子題

王氏祖訓二十條
一孝父母
一生衣食父恩深十月三年母艱辛夙夜常憂
因利欲沒天性
一敬兄弟
同氣連枝能有幾如何手足不相容成林竹木風
侮遺須親兄弟
一和夫婦
和氣同心宗道成鼎案如賓如瑟琴雞鳴戒旦足良配
把牝雞來報晨
一篤朋友

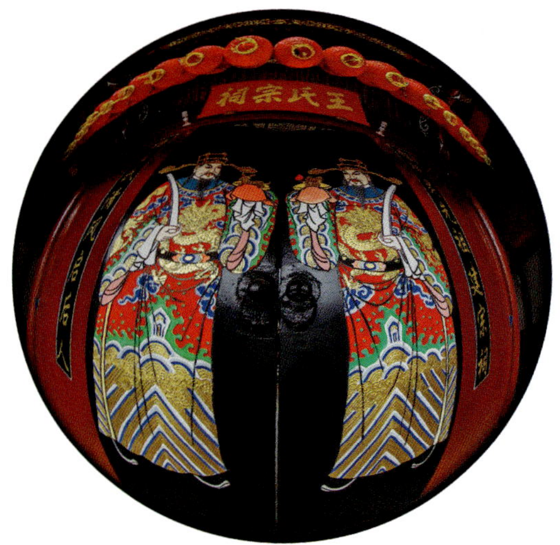
王氏宗祠

王氏宗祠

THE ANCESTRAL TEMPLE OF WANG

王氏宗祠

THE ANCESTRAL TEMPLE OF WANG

三槐堂
公元一九九四岁次甲戌年春节立
慎終追遠

王荣祠堂祭祀活动

THE RITUAL ACTIVITY OF WANG RONG'S ANCESTRAL TEMPLE

三槐堂
慎終追遠

西坑庙

THE XIKENG TEMPLE

观音庙

THE GUANYIN TEMPLE

佛日增輝

慈航普渡

隨處現身霞光充塞宇宙

若不回頭怎樣救苦救難

关王殿
GUAN WANG TEMPLE

天路

THE SKY ROAD TO THE VILLAGE

文化传承

TRADITIONAL CULTURAL INHERITANCE

鸟瞰上黄

A BIRD'S-EYE VIEW OF SHANGHUANG

贴春联
PASTING SPRING FESTIVAL COUPLETS

造火亮
MAKING LUNAR NEW YEARS EVE FIRE

订亲

ENGAGEMENT

五福临门
萬象更新

4507

古村老门

OLD DOORS IN THE ANCIENT VILLAGE

古村老门

OLD DOORS IN THE ANCIENT VILLAGE

古村百窗

OLD WINDOWS IN THE ANCIENT VILLAGE

古屋木雕构件

THE WOODCARVING COMPONENT OF AN ANCIENT HOUSE

传统村落民用家什

THE FURNITURE OF THE ANCIENT VILLAGE

灯芯盏

LAMPWICK HOLDER

风罩灯

LAMP

香盏

INCENSE

石磨

A STONE MILL

麻石

GRANITE

米斗
A RICE BOX

米筒
A RICE TUBE

茶筒
A TEA TUBE

壳篱
KELI

风车
A WINDMILL

刀架

A KNIFE REST

点心篮

A DESSERT BASKET

瓦质筷子笼

CERAMIC CHOPSTICKS HOLDER

石臼

THE STONE FOR MAKING RICE CAKES

靛青锄
A INDIGO HOE
靛青刀
A INDIGO KNIFE

蓑衣
PALM-BARK RAIN CAPE
笠帽
A RICE FARMER'S HAT

垒土墙工具
TOOLS FOR BUILDING COB WALLS

围帽

WEI HAT

安周帽

ANZHOU HAT

银扁簪

SILVER FLAT HAIRPIN

八卦镜

BAGUA MIRROR

肚兜

A BELLYBAND

木刻药方印刷版
WOOD ENGRAVED PRINTING PLATE
药书
A MEDINCE BOOK
朱砂碟
A CINNABAR DISH
墨水盒
NK CARTRIDGE
笔筒
A BRUSHPOD

古式家具

ANCIENT FURNITURE

王雄（WANG XIONG）（1925—1977），又名王亦平，曾在民国宣平县政府任宣传干事，有文才，善书法。

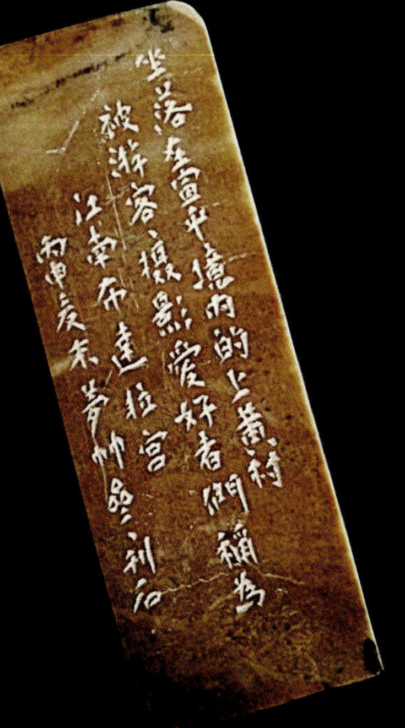

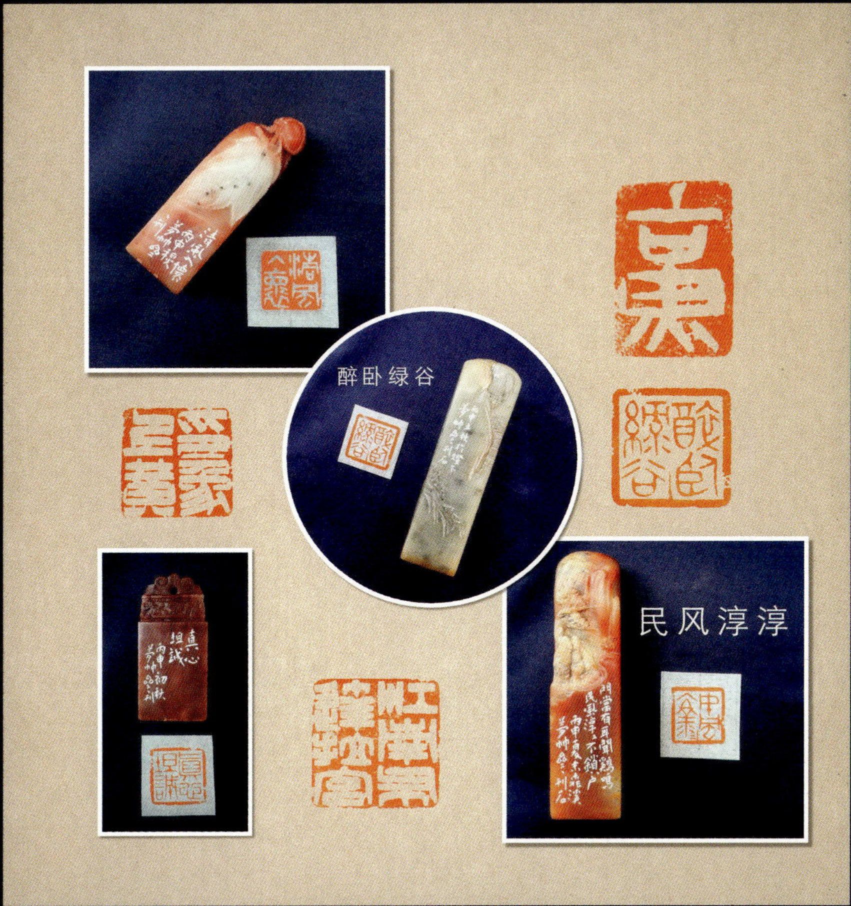

醉卧绿谷

民风淳淳

欲罷不能
昨晚散步时偶见此景憶寫之
王連水先武陽鎮
甲戌夏月

菊蔭雙禽
丙子年秋月
王連水写于
武义二职校

雞

雞羣
連水寫于甲戌年荷月

五雄圖
辛巳年春月
連水寫

王连水（WANG LIANSHUI）（1927—2013），教师，擅长书画，尤以写鸡及工楷见长。

ANCIENT PAINTINGS

同寿
甲戌荷月
連水写
秋耀金華
甲戌年夏連水作
不容丹桂稱前輩
只許寒梅步後塵
連水寫於甲戌夏月
瓜棚小景
連水写于甲戌夏
春江水暖
甲戌年春連水作
疎影橫斜
甲戌夏月
連水寫
俏不争春
乙亥年秋月王連水作

石娘娘（THE STONE MOTHER）

据上黄村民传说：早年的一个月夜，某先人因儿子突发腹疼，去村顶山上寻找草药。突然听见说话声。抬头远处，隐约见一个女人抱着一孩童哼着歌。先人继续前行，女人即站起隐没于旁边的一块巨石中。先人采药回来告知妻子，夫妻俩思前想后一夜，认定该女子是仙人化身。第二天即带着儿子去那石头面前跪下，祈求护佑。果不然儿子健康顺利成长，先人也每年按时前往祭拜。事情传开后，陆续有人前往祭拜并认巨石为干娘。历代相传，形成一种习俗文化。

孤魂祭坛（THE SACRIFICIAL ALTAR）

孤魂祭坛也称义祭坛，是义祭没有儿孙亡者之所。淹于荒草，任凭岁月风雨侵蚀，却承载着一段历史，代表着一种文化。体现上黄先人“老吾老以及人之老”的善举。

王德用祠堂祭谱

朝四壁降

农民哲言
THE VOWS OF FARMERS

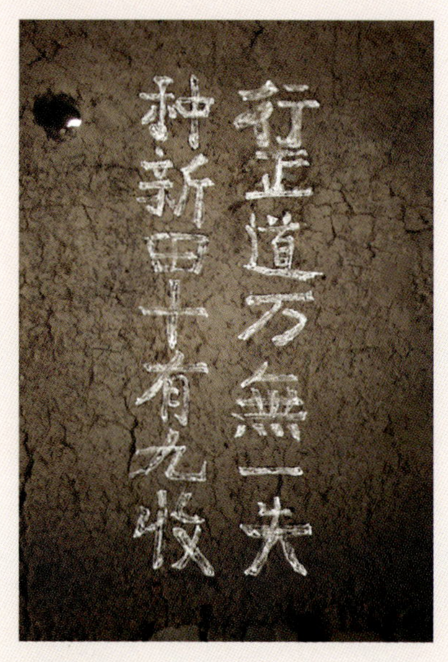

王清泉（WANG QINGQUAN）（1929—2005），农民，粗通文墨，能堪舆。

“行正道万无一失
种新田十有九收”

这是摄影人在上黄古道“石凉亭”土墙上发现并拍摄下来的。后经查证是已故老人王清泉在做护林员时所写的。该言道出了作为一个山区农民在纷繁复杂社会处世的人生真谛与大自然相处的经历体会，也是有着千年历史文化沉淀的古村落耕读传家的农民代表的真实写照。诗句朴实无华却字字玑珠，可谓是“农民哲言”。

田园景色

IDYLLIC SCENERY

初夏田园
COUNTRYSIDE IN EARLY SUMMER

春耕

SPRING PLOUGHING

忙作
BUSY FARM WORK

辛苦并快乐着

WORK HARD AND BE HAPPY

秋收

AUTUMN HARVEST

晒秋

DRY GRAIN IN THE SUN

含饴弄孙
（上黄双胞胎）
HAVING FUN WITH GRANDCHILDREN

花样童年

HAPPY CHILDHOOD

植树奖章上黄先人获知县奖励，王永平收藏。

A MEDAL FOR TREE PLANTING – THE ANCESTOR OF SHANGHUANG WON THE AWARD FROM COUNTRY MAGISTRATE (A COLLECTION OF WANG YONGPING)

王春田（WANG CHUNTIAN）（1927—），又名王师成，副主任医生，1948 年参军，1952 年进疆参加西北解放工作，后留疆直至 1992 年离休。

王有进（WANG YOUJIN）(1937—），1958 年参军入伍北海舰队，曾在中央军委工作，现转业退休。

云中部落

THE TRIBE IN THE CLOUD

名传八方

CIRCULATION IN ALL DIRECTIONS

简朴家风后代长传
勤劳美德儿孙永继

院士走访古村落

ACADEMICIANS VISITING THE ANCIENT VILLAGE

共商古村落保护

PLANNING FOR VILLAGE PROTECTION

记者采访
MEDIA REPORTING

中国科学院专家考察
VISITING BY EXPERTS OF CAS

欧美访客

VISITORS FROM EUROPE

上海小摄影师
THE PHOTOGRAPHER FROM SHANGHAI

喜见上黄
A DELIGHTED VISIT IN SHANGHUANG

后记

随着城市化的快速扩张，中国传统村落纷纷消失。坐落于大毛山有“江南布达拉宫”之称的千年古村落——上黄也受到了冲击。2015年，上黄村民王庆伟、王成亮等拉起了“幸福上黄”微信群，把散落在全国各地的上黄人牵连一处互通信息。有志于保护古村落的群友纷纷献计献策，成立了上黄古村落保护协会。由王永华、王建峰、王庆伟、王长伟、王长濂、王忠武等发起号召，捐款捐物出版《印象上黄》画册宣传古村落，让有千年历史的古村落辉煌再现。

2016年春节期间，武义县柳城畲族镇人民政府发起了最美古村落评比投票活动，王永华、王庆伟、王长伟、王忠武等发动上黄村村民、去过上黄的观光客人、喜爱上黄古村落的好友积极参与投票。上黄获得“最美古村落”称号。4月8日，上黄村迎来了千载难逢的喜庆，在金华市、武义县政府领导的陪同下，中国工程院蒋士成院士、郝吉明院士、段宁院士、朱利中院士以及在上黄出生长大的王金南院士和中国科学院等单位的知名专家学者莅临上黄，考察上黄村的古村落保护和农村环境保护。院士专家们被上黄村的优美自然环境和浓厚人文气息震撼，尤其是郝院士激动的言语哽咽其情景至今历历在目，期待古村落上黄在生态文明建设中脱颖而出。2016年上黄村好事连连，年底又入选为中国传统村落列入国家保护名单。游客纷至沓来，摄影爱好者络绎不绝。他们走古道、穿小巷、寻古渠、进五庙、爬毛山、上天池、观日出，将摄人心魄的风光人文瞬间定格，在世界各地微信朋友圈里展示着上黄古村落的美丽。

中国城市规划协会副会长、历史文化名城委员会副主任委员曹昌智教授多次亲临上黄考察古村落保护，指导编制上黄村传统村落保护发展规划。中国环境出版社高级编辑陈金华女士数次光临上黄村，对古村落自然风光、人文历史大加赞赏。解放军参谋王田大校利用假期光临上黄，也为她的美丽折服，制作格图宣传上黄厚重的人文气息和优美的自然风光。

在编辑《印象上黄》画册过程中，感谢温州摄影人吴焕亮先生的真诚，两次陪同画册主编高光荣先生到上黄取景；感谢陈金华女士热情指导《印象上黄》画册编辑工作，使我们从不懂到明白为什么这样做；感谢众多朋友，从世界和全国各地径直寻找到上黄，从不同视野拍摄了一幅幅精美的照片，让我们对自己家乡有了新的认识。要感谢的人很多，篇幅缘故不再一一赘述。

由于水平有限，谬误难免，敬请各界人士多多包涵并不吝指教。

《印象上黄》编委会
2017 年 12 月 18 日

POSTSCRIPT

With the expansion of urbanisation, traditional Chinese villages have been disappearing. The ancient village, Shanghuang, also known as "the Potala of the southern region of the Yangtze River", has also been affected. In 2015, villagers from Shanghuang: Wang Qingwei, Wang Chengliang and others formed a WeChat Group called "Happy Shanghuang" aiming to connect villagers all over China. Since then, Shanghuang people have been determined to protect the ancient village and established the Shanghuang Protection Association. Wang Yonghua, Wang Jianfeng, Wang Qingwei, Wang Changwei, Wang Changlian and Wang Zhongwu started a campaign, called *The Impression of Shanghuang* to present the glory of the ancient village to the world again.

During the Chinese Lunar New Year in 2016, The governor of Wuyi started a voting campaign for "the most beautiful ancient village". Wang Yonghua, Wang Qingwei, Wang Changwei and Wang Zhongwu called the actions of Shanghuang villagers and visitors vote for Shanghuang. Shanghuang eventually won the prize of "the most beautiful ancient village". On 8th April, Shanghuang welcomed an exciting honour. With the accompany of government officials of Jinhua and Wuyi, 5 academicians of Chinese Academy of Engineering: Jiang ShiCheng, Hao Jiming, Duan Ning, Zhu Lizhong and Wang Jinnan who was born and raised in Shanghuang, visited Shanghuang and investigated its natural habitat. The academicians were amazed by the natural beauty and humanity culture of Shanghuang, especially Academician Hao, who was utterly shocked by the beauty of Shanghuang. They sincerely wished Shanghuang can stand out from the construction of ecological civilisation. 2016 was a year full of joyful events—Shanghuang was also enlisted on the national protection list. Tourists and photographers keep visiting throughout the year. They walk along the ancient roads, across narrow allies; explore old canals and temples; climb the mountains to the sky pond. They captured the beauty of Shanghuang and shared on social media.

The vice president of China Association of City Planning and the Deputy Director of the Historical and Cultural Landmark Committee, Professor Cao Cangzhi has visited Shanghuang several times to provide guidances on the development of the protection plan for the ancient village. The senior editor of China Environment Press, Ms Chen Jinhua has also visited Shanghuang many times and highly appraised Its natural beauty and history. The senior colonel of People's Liberation Army, Wang Tian had his holiday here and was also impressed by Shanghuang's beauty and made posters to help the publicity of Shanghuang.

Special thanks to Mr Wu Huanliang, a photographer from Wenzhou, who came to shoot Shanghuang twice along with the editor of *The Impression of Shanghuang*, Mr Gao Guangrong. Sincere appreciation to Ms Chen Jinhua who actively advise on the editing of *The Impression of Shanghuang*. Thanks to the friends who travells far to Shanghuang. You bring us brand-new perspectives to our ancient home.

Editorial committee of *The Impression of Shanghuang*

18th December 2017